# WALKING TO WISDOM

LITERATURE GUIDE SERIES

# The Screwtape Letters

C.S. Lewis

by Kelly Warner

Inklings Collection

*Walking to Wisdom Literature Guide: The Screwtape Letters*


Version 1.1
ISBN: 978-1-60051-238-4



Classical Academic Press
515 S. 32nd Street
Camp Hill, PA 17011

www.ClassicalAcademicPress.com

Series Editor: Christine Perrin
Editor: Janet Dixon
Cover Design: Kristin Roach
Interior Design: Lenora Riley
Illustrations: Lauraine E. Robinson



PGP.02.22

# Walking to Wisdom Literature Guide: *The Screwtape Letters*

## Table of Contents

# INTRODUCTION TO STUDENTS

*Dear Students,*

We are excited that you have the privilege of reading *The Screwtape Letters* alongside a mentor (the writer of this guide) who will lead you "further up and further in" (C.S. Lewis's words in *The Last Battle*). We aim to give you a delightful experience with this book and, in the process, to share practices that we have learned that will help you become a good reader:

- reading carefully
- taking time to absorb a book
- paying attention to details as well as to great ideas over the whole book
- learning to mark up a book
- taking a few notes while reading
- learning to ask and answer good questions
- synthesizing those questions together in a piece of writing or an engaging project

If you spend a year doing all of the Inklings courses, you will not only collect some of the most important books and thoughts, but you will also have increased your abilities and pleasures as a reader.

C.S. Lewis, J.R.R. Tolkien, and Dorothy Sayers (two members and a friend of the Inklings whose work you will study in the Walking to Wisdom Literature Guides: The Inklings Collection) wrote nonfiction as well as fiction, and we begin your reading of fiction with a few select nonfiction essays they wrote on topics that overlap with the topics in the book you are reading. Part of their remarkable legacy is that they wrote about many of the same great ideas in stories, plays, poems, and nonfiction essays. This means that reading the ideas without the stories in these nonfiction works, or "context essays," will be a significant help to you in understanding them and in fully exploring the characters, plot, and imagery. American writer Flannery O'Connor said, "Our response to life is different if we have been taught only a definition of faith than if we have trembled with Abraham as he held a knife over Isaac." This is what stories do—they give us an experience of certain knowledge, which is why how we feel about the book is part of what the book is teaching us. We have kept these things in heart and mind while making this guide for you.

We have suggested two reading schedules—one that gives eleven days to study the book and the other that gives twenty-one days. Feel free to double that or add extra time for writing and enrichment activities (found at the end of the book). Your teacher will know what is best for your schedule. We have provided you with some space for answering questions, but we recommend that you also keep your thoughts, notes, and musings in a three-ring binder (or on the computer). For the Life Questions, you may want to keep a separate journal for meditative contemplation. We would like you to have as much room as you need, because you will find that the Inklings writers require a lot of space! It is highly recommended that you look up unfamiliar words found in C.S. Lewis's *The Screwtape Letters*, and keep a journal of these new vocabulary words and definitions as you work through the book and the guide.

You have the option of studying one guide or a few, or taking a year to study them all to fulfill your British literature requirement for high school English. Enjoy the study!

# Scope and Sequence for the Walking to Wisdom Literature Guides: The Inklings Collection

## C.S. Lewis

Context Essays* (selections from these are read at the beginning of each guide): excerpts from *Mere Christianity*,[1] *The Weight of Glory*,[2] *On Stories: And Other Essays on Literature*,[3] and "Theology in Stories" by Gilbert Meilaender[4]

- *The Lion, the Witch and the Wardrobe*[5]
- *The Last Battle*[6]
- *The Screwtape Letters*[7]
- *Till We Have Faces*[8]

## Dorothy Sayers

Context Essays*: excerpts from *Letters to a Diminished Church*[9]

*The Man Born to Be King* (twelve-play cycle integrating the four Gospels)[10]

## J.R.R. Tolkien

- *The Fellowship of the Ring*[11]
- *The Two Towers*[12]
- *The Return of the King*[13]

*Please note that the context essays are not supplied in this book. In the footnotes on this page we have supplied links that will guide you to where you can purchase or find the context essays. A PDF containing a list of all of the context essays and links to where you can purchase or find them is available at http://capress.link/wtwce01.

1. The Walking to Wisdom Literature Guides: The Inklings Collection is keyed to the following editions listed in these footnotes: C.S. Lewis, *Mere Christianity* (New York: HarperOne, 2009). **Available at https://amzn.to/2ImL1z9.**
2. C.S. Lewis, *The Weight of Glory* (New York: HarperOne, 2009). **Available at https://amzn.to/2Ii9BBa.**
3. C.S. Lewis, *On Stories: And Other Essays on Literature* (San Diego: Harcourt Books, 1966). **Available at https://amzn.to/2KpZXt7.**
4. Gilbert Meilaender, "Theology in Stories: C.S. Lewis and the Narrative Quality of Experience," *Word and World* 1/3 (1981): 222. **Available at http://wordandworld.luthersem.edu/content/pdfs/1-3_Experience/1-3_Meilaender.pdf.**
5. C.S. Lewis, *The Chronicles of Narnia* (New York: HarperCollins, 2001). **Available at https://amzn.to/2Imkan7.**
6. Lewis, *Chronicles.*
7. C.S. Lewis, *The Screwtape Letters* (New York: HarperOne, 2009). **Available at https://amzn.to/2jZrlTv.**
8. C.S. Lewis, *Till We Have Faces* (Orlando, FL: Harcourt, Brace, & Co., 1980). **Available at https://amzn.to/2IL0AA7.**
9. Dorothy Sayers, *Letters to a Diminished Church* (Nashville, TN: Thomas Nelson, 2004). **Available at https://amzn.to/2k0jIfF.**
10. Dorothy Sayers, *The Man Born to Be King: A Play-Cycle on the Life of Our Lord and Saviour Jesus Christ, Written for Broadcasting* (Grand Rapids, MI: Eerdmans, 1943). Reprinted with permission by Classical Academic Press, 2014. **Available at https://classicalacademicpress.com/product/the-man-born-to-be-king/.**
11. J.R.R. Tolkien, *The Fellowship of the Ring* (Boston: Mariner Books, 2005). **Available at https://amzn.to/2jZvEhm.**
12. J.R.R. Tolkien, *The Two Towers* (Boston: Mariner Books, 2005). **Available at https://amzn.to/2Gj7N5c.**
13. J.R.R. Tolkien, *The Return of the King* (Boston: Mariner Books, 2005). **Available at https://amzn.to/2L1JsVa.**

# The Inklings

The Inklings was an informal literary discussion group associated with the University of Oxford, England, for nearly two decades between the early 1930s and late 1949.[1] The Inklings were writers, including C.S. Lewis, J.R.R. Tolkien, and Charles Williams, who shared a love of similar stories and a remarkable commitment to ideas they shared. Their literary philosophies tended to depart from the period in which they were writing (modernist, 1900–1950) as did their cultural values. They liked to walk together and meet regularly to read their work aloud to one another.

"Properly speaking," wrote Warren Lewis (brother of C.S.), "the Inklings was neither a club nor a literary society, though it partook of the nature of both. There were no rules, officers, agendas, or formal elections."[2] While Dorothy Sayers did not attend the meetings herself, partly because she didn't live in the same town or teach at Oxford, some have called her an Inkling based on her friendship with Lewis and Charles Williams. Her correspondence with both was avid and their work concerned with many of the same subjects, characters, and plots. They were a great encouragement to one another. Lewis even read Sayers's play cycle, *The Man Born to Be King*, each year during the Lenten period. Therefore, although Sayers was not an "official" member of the Inklings, but rather a close friend of Lewis and Williams, we have included her in the Walking to Wisdom Literature Guides: The Inklings Collection, considering her an Inkling "in spirit," which is to say that she shared the same ideas and aspirations and engaged in similar writing projects. Had she lived in Oxford, we suspect she would have attended the informal meetings of this remarkable group.

Readings and discussions of the members' unfinished works were the principal purposes of meetings. Tolkien's *The Lord of the Rings*, Lewis's *Out of the Silent Planet*, and Williams's *All Hallows' Eve* were among the first novels the Inklings read to one another. Tolkien's fictional Notion Club (see *Sauron Defeated*) was based on the Inklings. Meetings were not all serious; the Inklings amused themselves by having competitions to see who could read notoriously bad prose for the longest without laughing.[3]

Until late 1949, Inklings readings and discussions usually occurred during Thursday evenings in C.S. Lewis's college rooms at Magdalen College. The Inklings and friends were also known to gather informally on Tuesdays at midday at a local public house, The Eagle and Child.

We hope that you will keep the spirit of the Inklings alive in your own study of this guide by working out your own responses to their work in community and conversation as well as laboring over your writing and sharing it with fellow travelers seeking to walk a similar path.

---

1. Clyde S. Kilby and Marjorie Lamp Mead, eds., *Brothers and Friends: The Diaries of Major Warren Hamilton Lewis* (San Francisco: Harper & Row, 1982), 230.
2. Bruce L. Edwards, *Apologist, Philosopher, and Theologian*, vol. 3 of *C.S. Lewis: Life, Works, and Legacy* (Westport, CT: Praegar, 2007), 279.
3. "War of Words over World's Worst Writer," *Culture Northern Ireland*, May 9, 2008, <http://www.culturenorthernireland.org/article/1739/war-of-words-over-world-s-worst-writer?search=inklings&rpg=1>.

# Daily Reading Outlines for C.S. Lewis's *The Screwtape Letters*

## Schedule 1

This schedule allows you to finish the book quickly. However, you will need significant time each day to devote to this heavier workload. This schedule also allows you to spend more time on final theme essays and enrichment activities when you finish the book.

Day 1: Context essay excerpts from *Mere Christianity:* "Charity" (Book III, chapter 9); "The Great Sin" (Book III, chapter 8); "Faith" (Book III, chapter 11).

Day 2: Context essay excerpts from *Mere Christianity:* "The Invasion" (Book II, chapter 2); "Time and Beyond Time" (Book IV, chapter 3)

Day 3: Preface; Chapters 1–3

Day 4: Chapters 4–7

Day 5: Chapters 8–11

Day 6: Chapters 12–16

Day 7: Chapters 17–20

Day 8: Chapters 21–25

Day 9: Chapters 26–27

Day 10: Chapters 28–31

Day 11: *Screwtape Proposes a Toast*

## Schedule 2

This schedule allows you more time to engage with the book as you read. You can spend more time on developing short answers to discussion questions, journal responses to life questions, or entries in a vocabulary journal. This schedule also allows more flexibility in time devoted daily to this assignment. Your teacher may give you still more time by adding a day or two to each segment.

Days 1–2: Context essay excerpts from *Mere Christianity:* "Charity" (Book III, chapter 9); "The Great Sin" (Book III, chapter 8); "Faith" (Book III, chapter 11)

Days 3–4: Context essay excerpts from *Mere Christianity:* "The Invasion" (Book II, chapter 2); "Time and Beyond Time" (Book IV, chapter 3)

Days 5–6: Preface; Chapters 1–3

Days 7–8: Chapters 4–7

Days 9–10: Chapters 8–11

Days 11–12: Chapters 12–16

Days 13–14: Chapters 17–20

Days 15–16: Chapters 21–25

Days 17–18: Chapters 26–27

Days 19–20: Chapters 28–31

Day 21: *Screwtape Proposes a Toast*

## Make Notes: Possess the Book

Becoming a reader is all about learning to pay attention and gather the details to relish and realize the significance and unity of what you are reading. Try using the following symbols or making up your own system that covers the same basics. Underline interesting passages. Write in the margins so that you can go back to reference what you wrote to make your Great Ideas Quotes pages, answer questions, hold discussions, and support points you make in your writing assignments. Here is a simple marking system that we have found effective:

- * This is important or delightful.
- ? I have a question.
- ?? I'm confused.
- ! This is surprising or exciting to me.
- T This could relate to one of the themes or motifs of the book.
- ✓ This relates to something else I have read.
- X This is part of the conflict or the problem of the story.
- C This is significant in defining this character.

## Tracing the Great Ideas

As you read, choose quotes related to the following great ideas topics (or themes) so that you can trace them all the way through the book. (Please remember that you are welcome to find your own great ideas themes in addition to ours.) Then be on the lookout for how they are worked out in each particular context. Some chapters may contain quotes relating to only one great ideas topic or to several topics. Write the quotes on the Great Ideas Quotes pages. (See page 8 for an example of how to record the quotations.) At the end of the guide you will reflect upon the themes of the course and choose one from which you will develop an argumentative essay. You may use our great idea definition for your essay's thesis or create a thesis of your own.

### Great Ideas

***Real pleasure:*** As God's invention, real pleasure serves God's purpose to replace lies with the truth of God's love for us as individuals and bring us into relationship with Him; pleasure brings us self-knowledge and humility, two conditions for coming into relationship with God.

***Evil/Twisting of the good:*** Satan succeeds in seducing our souls only when he can deceive us to accept a lesser substitute of what God has already graciously given.

***Relationships:*** Screwtape understands the important role relationships play in the patient's life and works to undermine the patient's faith through relationships.

***Time:*** Lewis illustrates his theory about God's perspective on time through the metaphor of a writer and his book.

***Gradual road to hell:*** C.S. Lewis argues that the most common and dangerous way for a person to wind up in hell is through small steps of disobedience, which she commits without any serious consideration of the consequences.

***Emotion and faith:*** Lewis argues that the changing nature and power of emotions can become a stumbling block for Christians, or can teach us to persevere through the peaks and troughs of our feelings.

***Individual soul:*** Lewis presents God as chiefly concerned with individual people, over and against nations, and committed to individuals becoming the fullest version of themselves.

### More background

The two truths that undergird C.S. Lewis's perspective on life are that individuals were created to be in relationship with God, and that the human soul exists for eternity. Lewis portrays Screwtape's equal awareness of these truths and characterizes him as desperate to destroy any person's relationship with God to ruin her eternal existence and union with God.

## Tell It Back

The method of narrating the chapters orally, or "telling it back," is a wonderful way to sum up the content of each chapter—with or without partners. You can even act out a chapter. This is a basic element of learning to read which never loses its delight and capacity to delight others. It also helps to develop a strong mental outlining ability. After each day's reading do an oral summary on a recording device or to another human being. If you are in a classroom setting, this is nicely done in groups where students coordinate what material they will share, in what sequence and in what amount of time. It should be a summary, hence shorter than it took to read it.

## Reading Questions

Reading questions encourage close reading of the text by asking comprehension questions. All answers are found in the text.

## Discussion Questions

Discussion questions require you to synthesize the main ideas of the text that may be either explicitly or implicitly stated. Your answers to these should explain Lewis's perspective, not your own. Depending on your level, learning needs, or preference, the in-depth discussion questions may be written as short answers (one to two paragraphs), discussed with the teacher/fellow students, or simply read to inspire critical thinking.

## Life Questions—Journaling Assignment

It's difficult to read any of C.S. Lewis's writing without thinking about applying his ideas to your own life. *The Screwtape Letters* is no exception. After each reading section, several "life questions" help you reflect on your own personal experiences and examine your own life in light of ideas from *The Screwtape Letters*. You may write informal responses to the life questions in a separate journal.

## Write Your Own Discussion Questions

At the end of each section, create two discussion questions that you think would make for good discussion among classmates, friends, and family. These should not chiefly be questions that have a sentence-long answer, but rather questions that would stimulate a longer exchange of ideas. Use our discussion questions and life questions as guides for writing yours.

## Chapter Summaries (Optional)

(This is optional, because you have already done this in oral or illustration form for the Tell It Back section. Whether or not you do it will depend on your teacher.) After reading each assigned chapter, summarize the main thematic arguments and significant plot details in two to five sentences (ours average one hundred words). A well-written summary concisely retells the most important ideas and events of the chapter. Avoid directly quoting or simply rephrasing sentences in your summaries. This exercise will strengthen your ability to consistently identify essential information from a text and retell this information without plagiarizing. Check the chapter summaries provided in the teacher's edition after you have attempted your own so that you can be sure you have covered the subject adequately. Summaries are also collected as an appendix in the teacher's edition (TE).

# INTRODUCTION TO *THE SCREWTAPE LETTERS*

In his book *The Art of Loving*, Erich Fromm articulates the human dread of isolation, of separateness, and describes how people handle the dread differently—some absorb weaker wills into their own, and some attach themselves to a stronger will in a symbiotic union, making themselves part of another person who directs them, guides them, and is their life. According to Fromm, love is the only way of knowledge—in the act of giving myself I find myself, I discover myself, I discover the beloved, I discover humankind. Self-transcendence—that is rising above the limited perspective and needs of one individual—has been a quest from the beginning of philosophy and of time. Different views of God, humans, and nature offer different answers about how we achieve this.

Lewis makes this issue of self-absorption versus self-giving or love the center of his Christian understanding; in any given moment we are either living by devouring another for our own benefit or out of our own ruling passions, or we are taking something that could have been ours and giving it to another for the benefit of another. The nearly unbelievable paradox of the Christian scriptures and life and the template that Christ laid down for us is that this giving is actually a receiving. This takes the "it is better to give than to receive" idea one step further—"to give is to receive."

Lewis demonstrates this radical idea of love and union with each other and with God in the negative in *The Screwtape Letters*. He shows the devouring nature of the fallen angels, or demonic creatures: even when they use terms of affection or endearment, the tempters are truly out for themselves only and always (even as an uncle or mentor). As the book goes on, the voice (Screwtape) becomes more menacing and more interested in absorbing the other will (Wormwood). Hell is noisy, devouring, competitive, and self-seeking, a place of separateness. (Or as Sartre says it: "Hell is the other.") Hell is also bureaucratic and grimy, the twisting of all that is good. It lacks creativity (as evil can only twist or imitate but cannot create); it is hungry and never full. Pride, which the Church has always considered the chief vice, and which leads to or undergirds all other vices, is central to this hellish approach to others and to oneself, as well as to God ("the complete anti-God state of mind," as Lewis calls it in *Mere Christianity*).

Lewis was absolutely insistent that nothing is automatic in life—that our will is totally involved in our direction and our eternal destiny; we participate with evil wills or with God's will, but we always have a choice. *The Screwtape Letters* provides unique insight into the battle to influence a person's choice. Screwtape's advice to the younger tempter reveals how to capitalize on different circumstances to persuade someone to join his will with hell's instead of submitting to God's will. This submission ties in to Lewis's discussion of the law of undulation with its troughs and peaks, as well as the matter of time. In chapter 6, Screwtape explains, "What the Enemy means by this [submitting] is primarily that he should accept with patience the tribulation which has actually been dealt out to him—the present anxiety and suspense. It is about *this* that he is to say 'Thy will be done,' and for the daily task of bearing *this* that the daily bread will be provided" (25). Further, in chapter 8, he explains that this daily surrendering happens under changing circumstances. Because we humans are both spirit and bodies, our experience is never completely steady but undulating. The law of undulation describes "the repeated return to a level from which they repeatedly fall back, a series of troughs and peaks . . . in every department of . . . life" (37). Screwtape explains that part of the Enemy's (God's) love for us is to give us perfect freedom, but this naturally involves us having to choose—to learn to believe and act even when our own animal and spiritual lives are sorely tempting us to forsake our faith (through exhaustion or loneliness). Screwtape notices:

> [God even] withdraws, if not in fact, at least from their conscious experience, all those supports and incentives. He leaves the creature to stand up on its own legs—to carry out from the will alone duties which have lost all relish. It is during such trough periods, much more than during the peak periods, that it is growing into the sort of creature He wants it to be. Hence the prayers offered in the state of dryness are those which please Him best. . . . He wants them to learn to walk and must therefore take away His hand. . . . He is pleased even with their stumbles. (40)

In a book told from the twisted and darkened point of view of the hellish tempter, the power of choice and active obedience to God still shines through. Screwtape worries, "Our cause is never more in danger than when a human, no longer desiring, but still intending, to do our Enemy's will, looks round upon a universe from which every trace of Him seems to have vanished, and asks why he has been forsaken, and still obeys" (40).

Another surprising aspect of Lewis's argument in this book is the emphasis on pleasure and pain as "unmistakably real, and therefore . . . a touchstone of reality" (64). Wormwood is severely chastised for allowing the patient to go on a walk and read a book he enjoys. Screwtape argues that pleasure and honest delight allows the patient to recover himself, to "come home" or to fully be himself. It remains Screwtape's desire to detach the patient from himself—the core of his unique and image-bearing selfhood—and thus detach him from God. True to the paradoxical skill of Lewis, the demon also explains that while the Enemy wants to detach humans from "the clamor of self-will" (65), the deepest likings and impulses of any person are the raw material, the starting point, the distinctness out of which a relationship to God grows and blossoms and yields fruit.

Because of this, Screwtape bemoans, "The man who truly and disinterestedly enjoys any one thing in the world, for its own sake, and without caring two-pence what other people say about it, is by that very fact forearmed against some of our subtlest modes of attack" (66). He goes on to say that cricket, stamp collecting, cocoa, and even tripe and onions have a power to ward off social temptation and has a sort of humility and self-forgetfulness to it that has a spiritual relevance. Augustine (Bishop of Hippo), who influenced Lewis, also discusses the fact that we are what we love, and that formation of our loves is essential to our personhood and our faith. Faith is not a stepping out of our particular selves, but moving more deeply into it toward our Maker. Yet Screwtape is still hopeful that the patient will recover from the moment of pleasure. His best advice for salvaging the patient once he has come closer to himself is to be sure he doesn't take any action that corresponds to this revelation.

All human action takes place in a linear stream of time. Through *The Screwtape Letters*, Lewis redefines our conception of time: Screwtape often advises Wormwood to take advantage of the patient's limited understanding of it. Because He destined people for eternity, God intends us to be concerned with two things: eternity itself and the present. Since the present best reflects the freedom and actuality of eternity, Screwtape encourages Wormwood to have the patient focus on the past, or especially the future—which is pure conjecture and therefore completely unreal. Lewis thus clarifies our experience of time, but also moves toward explaining God's perspective. God's actions (and answers to prayer) are not chained by adherence to a linear progression of time. Moreover, His experience of time protects the integrity of human will and action: "the Enemy does not *foresee* the humans making their free contributions in a future, but sees them doing so in His unbounded Now. And obviously to watch a man doing something is not to make him do it" (150).

C.S. Lewis's *The Screwtape Letters* parades us through the unfamiliar and the both laughable and sickening mind of a demon dedicated to human destruction. The jarring reversal of values and hellishly bureaucratic diction forces us to abandon our typical perspective and interpretive lens for religious literature. And on this voyage through dark spirits, Lewis not only entertains us (or frightens us) with hell's perspective, but also awakens our hearts to heaven's reality. *The Screwtape Letters* pushes its readers to confront our often confused and limited perception of reality and, from this new awareness, challenges us to choose to act upon what is true.

## For Further Biographical Study

Please see the following resource: http://www.cslewis.org/resource/chronocsl/. This website—created by the C.S. Lewis Foundation—suggests and links to a number of other excellent sources.

# Tracing the Great Ideas

You may record your Great Ideas Quotes on the pages that follow or you may want to consider placing copies of the Great Ideas Quotes pages in a three-ring notebook at the beginning of your guide work to keep a "map" of your reading.

You should feel free to shorthand quotes by listing the quote's beginning and end, then its page number, on the proper Great Ideas Quotes page.

## Examples:

**Great Ideas Quotes throughout the book for the theme *Relationships***

"When he gets to his pew and looks round him he sees just that selection of his neighbours whom he has hitherto avoided. You want to lean pretty heavily on those neighbours. Make his mind flit to and fro between an expression like 'the body of Christ' and the actual faces in the next pew." (Chapter 2, pg. 6)

**shorthand version:**

"when he gets to his . . . next pew." (6)

"Make sure that they [his prayers for his mother] are always very 'spiritual,' that he is always concerned with the state of her soul and never wither her rheumatism." (Chapter 3, pg. 12)

**shorthand version:**

"make sure that . . . her rheumatism." (12)

"When two humans have lived together for many years it usually happens that each has tones of voice and expressions of face which are almost unendurably irritating to the other. Work on that." (Chapter 3, pg. 13)

**shorthand version:**

"when two humans have lived together. . . . Work on that." (13)

## Great Ideas Quotes throughout the Book for the Theme *Real Pleasure*

## Great Ideas Quotes throughout the Book for the Theme *Evil/Twisting the Good*

# Great Ideas Quotes throughout the Book for the Theme *Relationships*

# Great Ideas Quotes throughout the Book for the Theme *Time*

# Great Ideas Quotes throughout the Book for the Theme *Gradual Road to Hell*

# Great Ideas Quotes throughout the Book for the Theme *Emotion and Faith*

# Great Ideas Quotes throughout the Book for the Theme *Individual Soul*

# SUMMARIZE THE CONTEXT ESSAYS: *MERE CHRISTIANITY* EXCERPTS

Before you start *The Screwtape Letters*, you will read and summarize the excerpts from *Mere Christianity* we have selected. Then cross-check your summaries with ours (in the teacher's edition) to make sure you have covered the topic adequately. Our summaries range from 50–125 words, but your teacher will assign a word count for yours. These "context essays" will help you to understand and gain insight into many of the ideas that arise in *The Screwtape Letters*. An important part of becoming a good reader involves being able to summarize your reading in such a way that someone else can understand what you have read.

## "Charity" Summary (from *Mere Christianity*, Book III, Chapter 9)

## "The Great Sin" Summary (from *Mere Christianity*, Book III, Chapter 8)

"Faith" Summary (from *Mere Christianity*, Book III, Chapter 11)

"The Invasion" Summary (from *Mere Christianity*, Book II, Chapter 2)

"Time and Beyond Time" Summary (from *Mere Christianity*, Book IV, Chapter 3)

# Unit 1: Preface; Chapters 1–3

## Make Notes in Your Book*

Don't forget to make notes in your book!

## Tracing the Great Ideas*

Find quotes in these chapters that relate to the great ideas, or themes. Write down the quote with its page number on the corresponding Great Ideas Quotes pages provided (at the beginning of this guide). Keeping track of quotes will help you write the final theme essays!

### Example quotes and their themes

**Great Ideas Quotes throughout the book for the theme *Relationships***

"I do not mean the Church . . . tempters uneasy" (5).

"When he gets to his . . . next pew" (6).

**Great Ideas Quotes throughout the book for the theme *Gradual road to hell***

"Even if a particular train of thought . . . the stream" (2).

"Keep pressing home . . . of things" (4).

**Great Ideas Quotes throughout the book for the theme *Individual soul***

"The history of the European War . . . to Screwtape" (x).

## Tell It Back*

Do an oral summary of your reading on a recording device or to another human being. Narrate the most important events in order while sharing the elements of the characters' development that are important.

## Reading Questions

1. In the first letter, Screwtape says that people no longer think about doctrines as true or false, but use other adjectives. What are some of these adjectives?

______________________________

______________________________

______________________________

______________________________

*You'll see these icons at the beginning of each unit as reminders to make notes, trace great ideas, and tell back what you've read.

2. On page 5, Screwtape describes two different meanings of the word "church." What are these two meanings?

______________________________________________

______________________________________________

______________________________________________

______________________________________________

______________________________________________

______________________________________________

3. Who does the patient live with?

______________________________________________

______________________________________________

## Discussion Questions

1. In the preface to *The Screwtape Letters*, C.S. Lewis explains two errors people make when considering the issue of devils. Identify each view. Then, from your own knowledge and the excerpt "The Invasion" from *Mere Christianity*, explain why Lewis believes Christians should avoid both these views.

2. According to these chapters, how do reason and emotion affect spiritual development?

3. Screwtape reveals prayer can be stripped of its power. How?

## Life Questions—Journaling Assignment

Feel free to respond to the life questions here or to keep them in a separate journal used for meditative contemplation.

1. Screwtape encourages Wormwood to focus the patient on other people's faults (such as other people at church and his own mother) without recognizing his own sinful situation or habits that annoy other people. Examine your own life. Are there areas of life in which you are quick to point out the flaws of others? Does this habit help or hurt your enjoyment of life and relationships?

2. Examine your own prayer habits. What satisfies you about your prayer life and what do you feel is lacking? Have you ever found yourself falling into the unhelpful habits that Screwtape encourages?

## Write Your Own Discussion Questions

1. 

2. 

## Chapter Summaries

Write your own chapter summaries here or in your binder and then cross-check them with the summaries in the teacher's edition.

**Preface:**

**Chapter 1:** ____________________

**Chapter 2:** ____________________

**Chapter 3:** ____________________

# Unit 2: Chapters 4–7

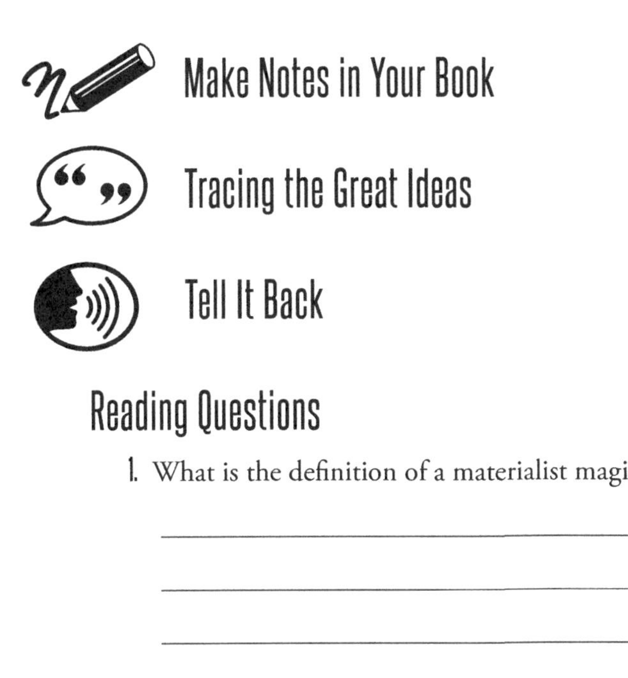


## Reading Questions

1. What is the definition of a materialist magician?

2. How does prayer "practiced by those who are very far advanced in the Enemy's service" seem similar to the prayer of new "clever and lazy patients" (16)?

3. Does Screwtape wish more people would die in nursing homes or that more people would die during a war?

## Discussion Questions

1. According to these chapters, how can prayer be turned into idolatry?

2. Are major world events really important? Compare and contrast Wormwood's and Screwtape's perspectives on the World War II.

3. Why does Screwtape hope to produce a materialist magician? Use the definition from reading question 1 to help you answer this question.

4. Why does Screwtape consider including patriotism or pacifism as part of his religion detrimental to the patient's faith?

## Life Questions—Journaling Assignment

Feel free to respond to the life questions here or to keep them in a separate journal used for meditative contemplation.

1. In letter 6, ST urges the junior demon to encourage the patient to hate the people with whom he comes into contact daily and to redirect any good and kind thoughts his patient might have toward people far away from his everyday life—those people the patient may not even know. Who are the closest people in your life, and how do you treat them? Have you been treating those close to you badly while imagining you are doing good to people you don't know? How do your actions toward those closest to you measure up to how you believe you should live?

2. Screwtape demonstrates in letter 7 how adding other ideas to Christianity (in the patient's case, pacifism or patriotism) can cause these other ideas to become more important than the core message of Christianity. In the Christian world today and in your own life, what ideas do you see commonly added to Christianity? In your own experience, how do these experiences affect one's personal faith and the Church as a whole?

## Write Your Own Discussion Questions

1. ______________________________________________

______________________________________________

2. ______________________________________________

______________________________________________

## Chapter Summaries

Write your own chapter summaries here or in your binder and then cross-check them with the summaries in the teacher's edition.

**Chapter 4:** ______________________________________________

**Chapter 5:** ______________________________________________

**Chapter 6:** ______________________________________________

Chapter 7: ___

# Unit 3: Chapters 8–11

## Make Notes in Your Book

## Tracing the Great Ideas

## Tell It Back

## Reading Questions

1. In the essay "Faith" (the excerpt from *Mere Christianity* you read before you began *The Screwtape Letters*), Lewis provides three real-life examples of emotion affecting a person's faith in something ordinary. What is one of the examples?

2. Screwtape describes humans as amphibians on page 37. What does he mean?

3. The patient meets a middle-aged married couple at his office. What information does Screwtape give about their character?

## Discussion Questions

1. Explain the law of undulation. How does this relate to a Christian's spiritual development?

2. Why are friendships important to spiritual development? (Consider the temptation to create parallel lives and the role of pride.)

3. Describe the four different types of laughter, and provide examples of each from your own life. Which types does Screwtape consider dangerous or beneficial to his own cause? Has this been the case in your observation?

   a.

b. ____________________________________________

____________________________________________

____________________________________________

____________________________________________

c. ____________________________________________

____________________________________________

____________________________________________

____________________________________________

d. ____________________________________________

____________________________________________

____________________________________________

____________________________________________

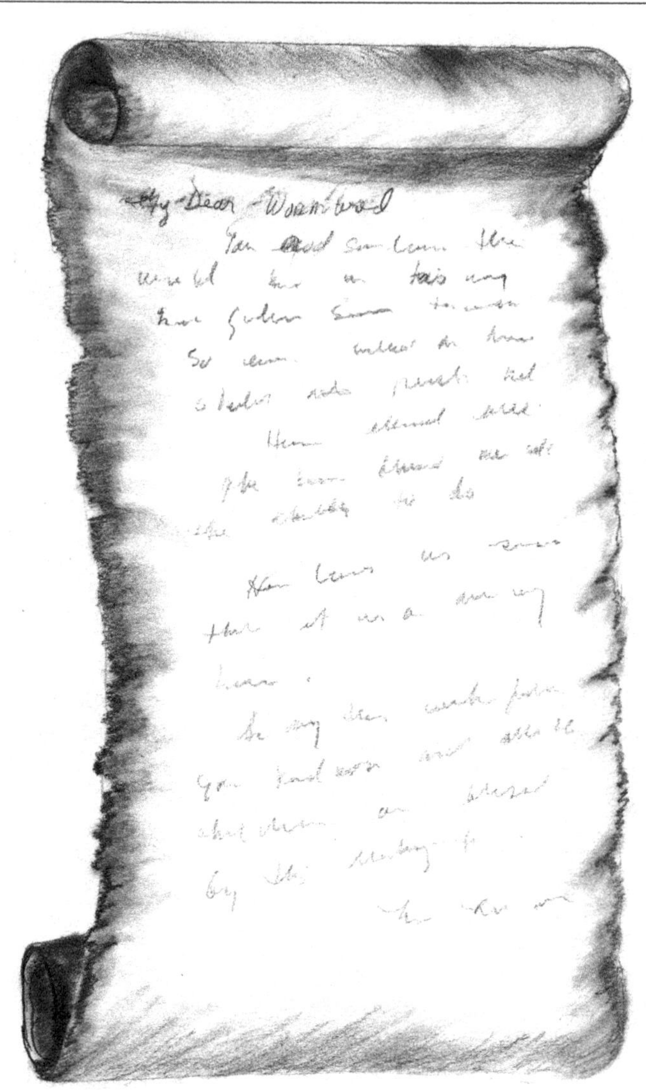

## Life Questions—Journaling Assignment

Feel free to respond to the life questions here or to keep them in a separate journal used for meditative contemplation.

1. In what ways have you noticed the law of undulation in your own life? Does recognizing the natural ups and downs of spiritual life encourage you or discourage you? Why?

2. Screwtape notes that friendships can greatly influence the patient's life. Consider your own friends. How have your friends influenced your beliefs and actions? Do your friends have a positive or negative impact on your spiritual development?

## Write Your Own Discussion Questions

1.

2.

## Chapter Summaries

Write your own chapter summaries here or in your binder and then cross-check them with the summaries in the teacher's edition.

**Chapter 8:**

Chapter 9:

Chapter 10:

Chapter 11:

# Unit 4: Chapters 12–16

Make Notes in Your Book

Tracing the Great Ideas

Tell It Back

## Reading Questions

1. Why is Screwtape glad in letter 12 that the patient still attends church?

2. What protects the patient from Wormwood's attack during his walk back from the old mill (63)?

3. Which of the three—past, present, or future—is most like eternity?

## Discussion Questions

1. According to Screwtape, what is the role of pleasure in temptation?

2. In letter 13, Screwtape writes, "The characteristic of Pains and Pleasures is that they are unmistakably real, and therefore, as far as they go, give the man who feels them a touchstone of reality." Explain why pain and pleasure, as "touchstones of reality," present a problem for Screwtape and Wormwood?

3. God desires people to be humble. Describe God's version of humility and Screwtape's corrupted version of humility. According to these chapters, how does a correct definition of humility help Christians live a life more pleasing to God?

4. Describe the different relationships between the present, the past, and the future with eternity. How should a Christian approach the concept of time? What difference should this make in the way we live our lives?

## Life Questions—Journaling Assignment

Feel free to respond to the life questions here or to keep them in a separate journal used for meditative contemplation.

1. What temptations have you experienced in your life? What makes these sins tempting? How do you withstand temptation?

2. What do you think about the virtue of humility? How does a humble attitude differ from self-esteem? In your own life, how can you show humility? How has an experience of your own pride or humility (or that of another) instructed you?

## Write Your Own Discussion Questions

1. 

2. 

## Chapter Summaries

Write your own chapter summaries here or in your binder and then cross-check them with the summaries in the teacher's edition.

**Chapter 12:**

Chapter 13: ______________________________

**Chapter 14:** ________________________________

**Chapter 15:** ________________________________

**Chapter 16:** ________________________________

# Unit 5: Chapters 17–20

Make Notes in Your Book

Tracing the Great Ideas

Tell It Back

## Reading Questions

1. Screwtape asks Wormwood if he has shown his letters to anyone. What is Screwtape concerned about in his letters?

2. Why does the patient's mother have a hard time finding domestic help or friends who can cook her meals?

3. Screwtape requests a report about a certain group of people in the patient's neighborhood. What is the group?

## Discussion Questions

1. What types of gluttony does Screwtape explain? How do both of these sinful attitudes cause destruction in people's lives?

2. Why can Screwtape not understand God's interest in having a relationship with humans?

3. Screwtape insists that being in love and marriage are neither good nor bad. Why does he believe this? Do you agree?

4. According to these chapters, how do culture and society influence individual experiences of love and sexuality?

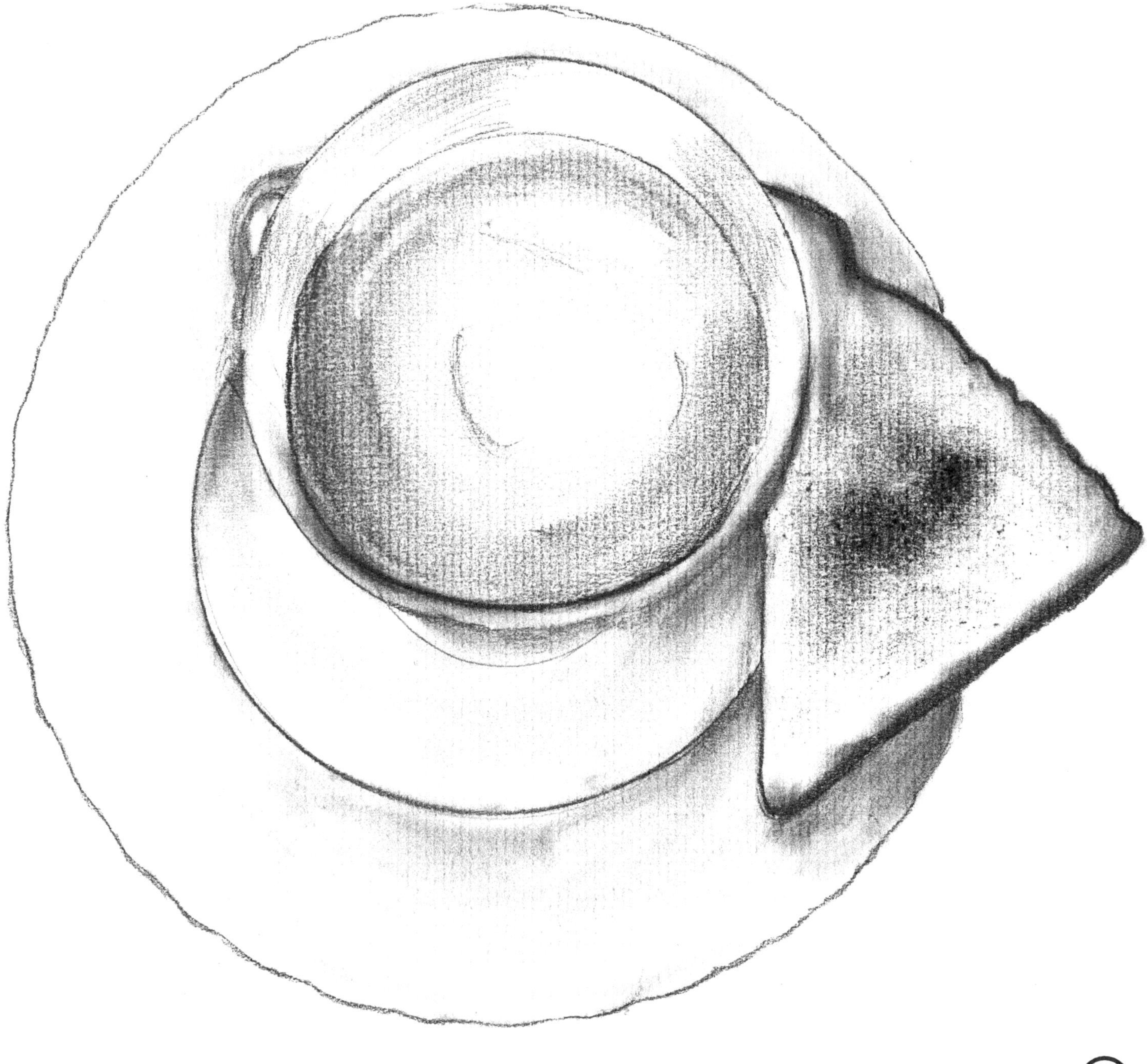

## Life Questions—Journaling Assignment

Feel free to respond to the life questions here or to keep them in a separate journal used for meditative contemplation.

1. From television, movies, magazines, and the Internet, we constantly see images and hear stories about what love is and looks like. What do Photoshopped and airbrushed models in advertisements say about beauty? What do popular television shows and romantic comedies say about culture's view of relationships? How do these depictions of beauty and relationships influence you? How do they influence your friends?

2. Screwtape talks about two types of gluttony: the gluttony of excess (having too much) and the gluttony of delicacy (wanting things a certain way). Have you noticed a tendency toward one of these types of gluttony in your life? If so, where do you see this gluttony (it doesn't have to be in matters of food!)? How can you change this attitude? What sorts of gluttony does our own culture perpetuate?

## Write Your Own Discussion Questions

1. 

2. 

## Chapter Summaries

Write your own chapter summaries here or in your binder and then cross-check them with the summaries in the teacher's edition.

**Chapter 17:** ______________________________

**Chapter 18:** ______________________________

**Chapter 19:** ______________________________

**Chapter 20:** ______________________

# Unit 6: Chapters 21–25

Make Notes in Your Book

Tracing the Great Ideas

Tell It Back

## Reading Questions

1. Why does Screwtape consider laughable human claims to own anything?

2. Screwtape is upset that Wormwood tried to get him in trouble with the secret police. What booklet does Screwtape send Wormwood as a warning?

3. The patient's girlfriend has a personality flaw that makes her think nonbelievers are stupid or ridiculous. Although hers is a small sin arising from naïveté, Screwtape hopes the patient will imitate and exaggerate this characteristic. This exaggeration will turn into what vice?

## Discussion Questions

1. What is wrong with the pronoun "mine"?

2. Why does Screwtape turn into a centipede? What does this imply about Screwtape's spiritual condition? What do you think about the metaphor?

3. Letters 23–25 each explain a different way to corrupt faith (historical Jesus, spiritual pride, and Christianity And). How does each of these corrupting strategies work? What do they have in common with each other?

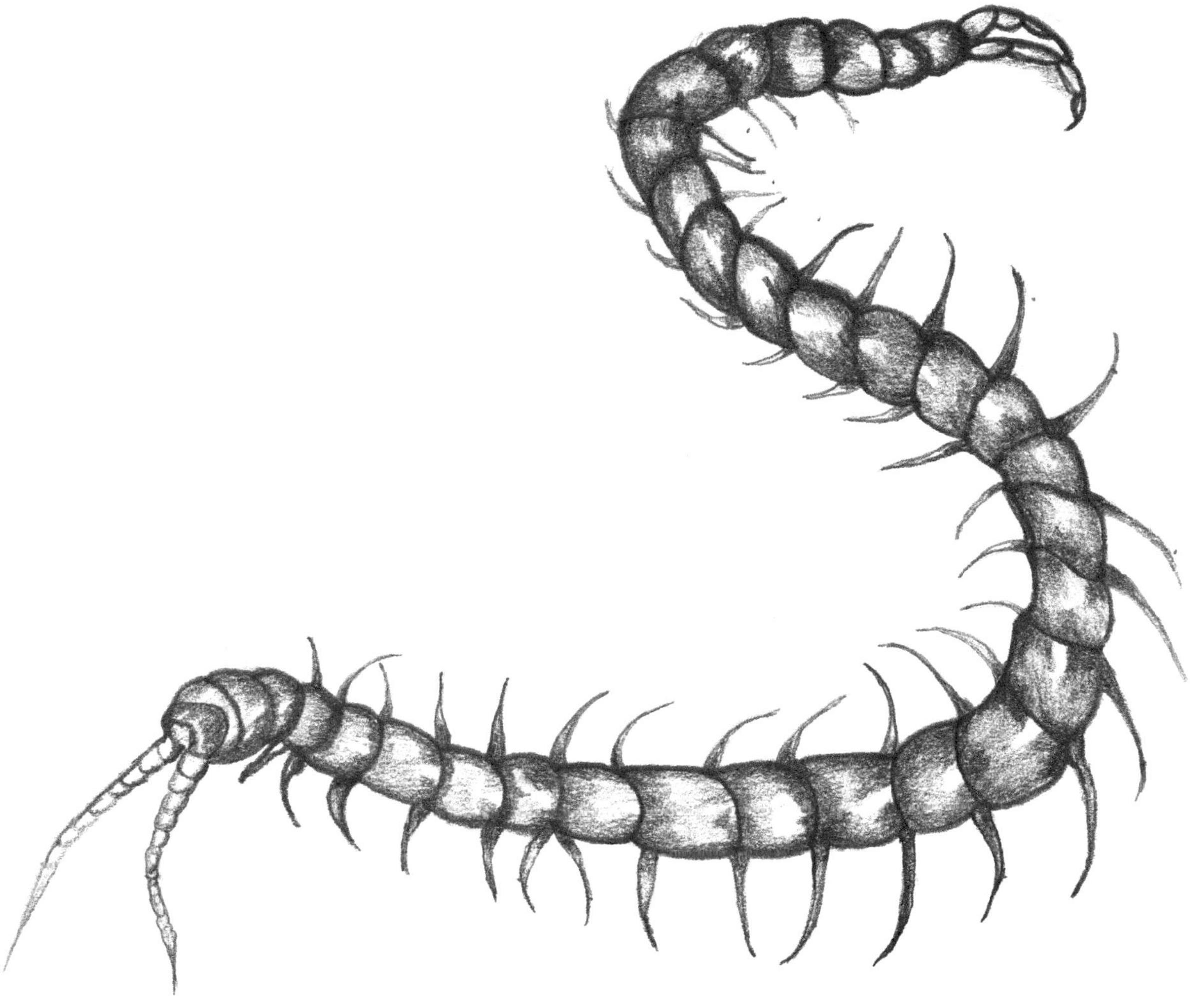

## Life Questions—Journaling Assignment

Feel free to respond to the life questions here or to keep them in a separate journal used for meditative contemplation.

1. What do you call "mine"? Does this word "mine" always mean the same thing? How do you understand your use of the word "mine" in light of God's sovereignty (ownership) over all He has made? How might that influence your use of your own things? How do we both steward (act as good guardians of) our material things and share them?

2. Screwtape explains three different ways to corrupt faith in these chapters (historical Jesus, spiritual pride, and Christianity And). Give examples from your own life of one or more of these faith-corrupting ideas. How do you think a Christian could stand up to these strategies?

## Write Your Own Discussion Questions

1. 

2. 

## Chapter Summaries

Write your own chapter summaries here or in your binder and then cross-check them with the summaries in the teacher's edition.

**Chapter 21:**

Chapter 22: ______________________________

Chapter 23: ______________________________

Chapter 24: ______________________________________________

Chapter 25: ______________________________________________

# Unit 7: Chapters 26–27

Make Notes in Your Book

Tracing the Great Ideas

Tell It Back

## Reading Questions

1. In the essay "Time and Beyond Time" (the excerpt from *Mere Christianity* you read before you began *The Screwtape Letters*), what metaphor (comparison) does Lewis use to describe how God is outside of our earthly, linear time line?

2. Screwtape labels "unselfishness" a negative substitute for a positive virtue of the Enemy's (God's). What is this virtue? How would you describe it?

3. Screwtape notes that modern people ask questions about who influenced ancient writers, what phase in the author's development the writing depicts, and how it has been understood or interpreted by people. What question do people not ask?

## Discussion Questions

1. Compare our human experience of time to God's experience of time, according to Lewis. Use the excerpt "Time and Beyond Time" to help answer the question.

2. What is the difference between selflessness and unselfishness? In what ways does unselfishness seep into relationships, and what is the result?

3. Why does Screwtape believe that prayer requests that God chooses to grant and chooses not to grant can both be used to undermine the patient's belief in the power of prayer?

## Life Questions—Journaling Assignment

Feel free to respond to the life questions here or to keep them in a separate journal used for meditative contemplation.

1. Remember an experience in your life when someone's unselfish actions caused problems. Imagine if this person decided to act selflessly instead, and describe how you think things would have turned out differently.

2. How do you respond when God chooses to grant a prayer request? How do you respond when He chooses not to grant one? How do God's answers to your prayers affect your faith?

## Write Your Own Discussion Questions

1.

2.

## Chapter Summaries

Write your own chapter summaries here or in your binder and then cross-check them with the summaries in the teacher's edition.

**Chapter 26:**

**Chapter 27:** ______________________________________________

Make Notes in Your Book

Tracing the Great Ideas

Tell It Back

## Reading Questions

1. What is the definition of courage, according to letter 29?

2. How does the patient die?

3. What does Screwtape hope happens to Wormwood now that his patient has died?

## Discussion Questions

1. Why would Screwtape prefer a Christian to live a long life?

2. How can cowardice be used to bring people to God?

3. Explain how Screwtape hopes to use the patient's emotional response to the horrors and destructions of war to attack his faith.

## Life Questions—Journaling Assignment

Feel free to respond to the life questions here or to keep them in a separate journal used for meditative contemplation.

1. Can you recall a time when you acted courageously, based on Lewis's definition of courage in letter 29? What happened? Why was it difficult to choose virtue in that situation? What helped you make the courageous decision?

2. Have you ever done something cowardly, according to the same definition of courage? Why was it difficult to choose virtuously in that situation? How can God transform this experience of cowardice into something that glorifies Him?

## Write Your Own Discussion Questions

1. 

2. 

## Chapter Summaries

Write your own chapter summaries here or in your binder and then cross-check them with the summaries in the teacher's edition.

**Chapter 28:** ______________________________

Chapter 29: ______________________________

Chapter 30: ______________________________

Chapter 31: ______________________________

# UNIT 9: *SCREWTAPE PROPOSES A TOAST*

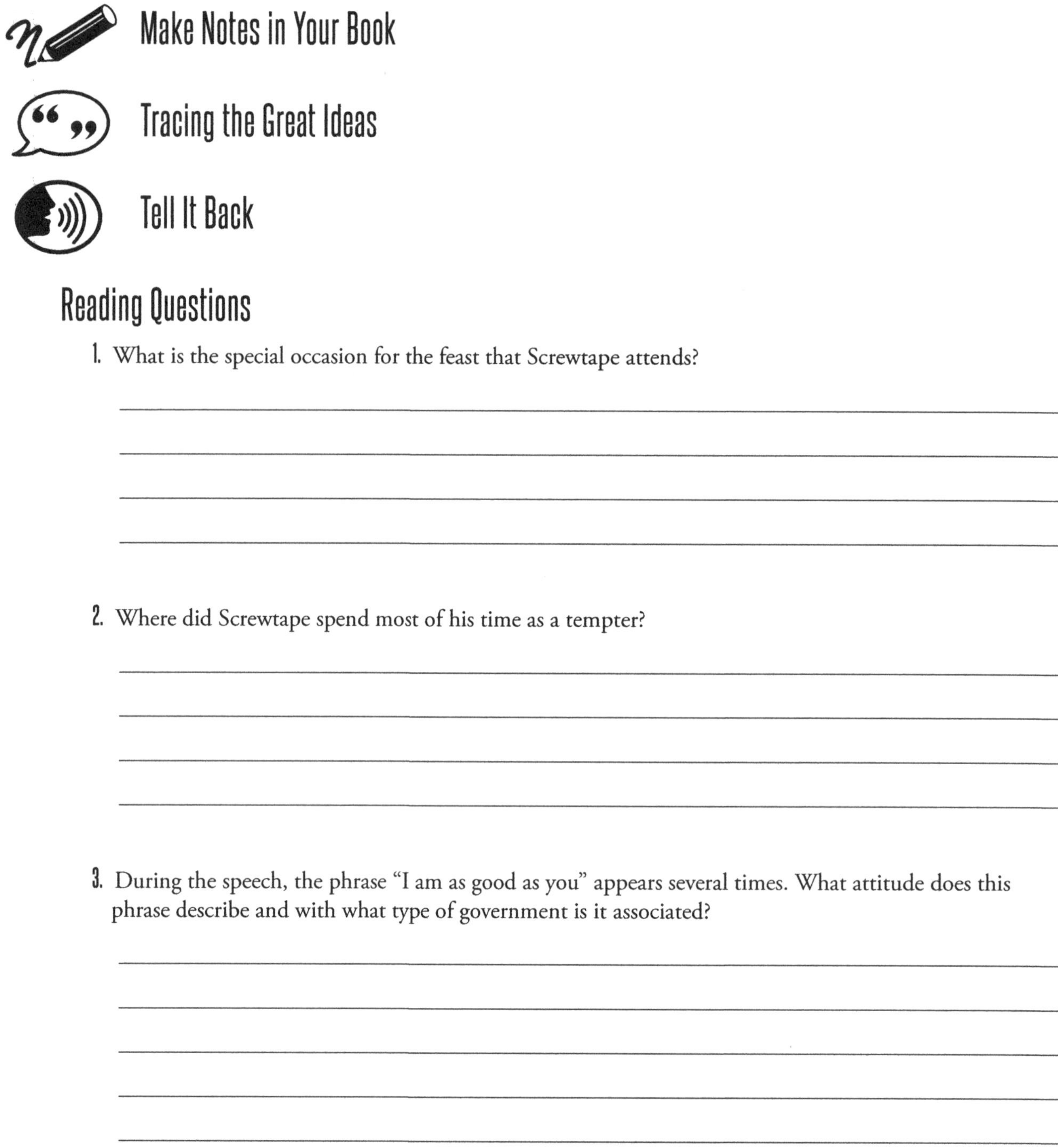

## Make Notes in Your Book

## Tracing the Great Ideas

## Tell It Back

## Reading Questions

1. What is the special occasion for the feast that Screwtape attends?

2. Where did Screwtape spend most of his time as a tempter?

3. During the speech, the phrase "I am as good as you" appears several times. What attitude does this phrase describe and with what type of government is it associated?

# Discussion Questions

1. Screwtape acknowledges that their feasts today are different from the past. What is different about the souls they devour today?

2. What is the relationship between historical events and spiritual states, according to the demons?

3. Why are Pharisees a special vintage?

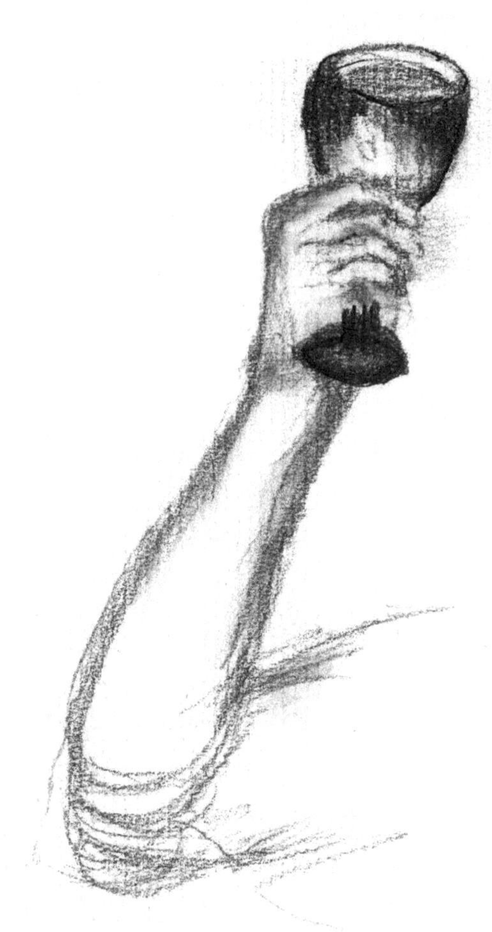

## Life Questions—Journaling Assignment

Feel free to respond to the life questions here or to keep them in a separate journal used for meditative contemplation.

1. Screwtape argues that even though the quality of sinners has decreased, the quality of saints has also decreased. Do you think it is true? Do you think there are fewer fully devoted Christians now than in previous times? Do you see yourself as a passionate Christian? Why or why not?

2. Do you see a relationship between events in the world right now and people's spiritual states?

## Write Your Own Discussion Questions

1.

2.

## Chapter Summary

Write your own chapter summary here or in your binder and then cross-check it with the summaries in the teacher's edition.

***Screwtape Proposes a Toast:***

# Quotation Identification

We have chosen memorable quotations that are significant to *The Screwtape Letters*. These quotations are all spoken by Screwtape and summarize some of the major ideas in the book and in Lewis's work at large. Give a few sentences that describe the context of the quote in the themes of this book.

## Unit 1 (Chapter 2)

Desiring their freedom, He therefore refuses to carry them, by their mere affections and habit, to any of the goals which He sets before them: He leaves them to "do it on their own."

## Unit 2 (Chapter 4)

If this fails, you must fall back on a subtler misdirection of his intention. Whenever they are attending to the Enemy Himself we are defeated, but there are ways of preventing them from doing so. The simplest is to turn their gaze away from him towards themselves.

## Unit 3 (Chapter 8)

One must face the fact that all the talk about His love for men, and His service being perfect freedom, is not (as one would gladly believe) mere propaganda, but an appalling truth. He really *does* want to fill the universe with a lot of loathsome little replicas of Himself—creatures whose life, on its miniature scale, will be qualitatively like His own, not because He has absorbed them but because their wills freely conform to His. We want cattle who can finally become food; He wants servants who can finally become sons. We want to suck in, He wants to give out. We are empty and would be filled; He is full and flows over.

## Unit 4 (Chapter 14)

The Enemy wants to bring the man to a state of mind in which he could design the best cathedral in the world, and know it to be the best, and rejoice in the fact, without being any more (or less) or otherwise glad at having done it than he would if it had been done by another. The Enemy wants him, in the end, to be free from any bias in his own favour that he can rejoice in his own talents as frankly and gratefully as in his neighbour's talents—or in a sunrise, an elephant, or a waterfall. He wants each man, in the long run, to be able to recognise all creatures (even himself) as glorious and excellent things. He wants to kill their animal self-love as soon as possible; but it is His long-term policy, I fear, to restore to them a new kind of self-love—a charity and gratitude for all selves, including their own; when they have really learned to love their neighbours as themselves, they will be allowed to love themselves as their neighbours.

## Unit 5 (Chapter 18)

The whole philosophy of Hell rests on recognition of the axiom that one thing is not another thing, and, specially, that one self is not another self. My good is my good and your good is yours. What one gains another loses . . . "To be" *means* "to be in competition."

## Unit 6 (Chapter 22)

Music and silence—how I detest them both! How thankful we should be that ever since Our Father entered Hell—though longer ago than humans, reckoning in light years, could express—no square inch of infernal space and no moment of infernal time has been surrendered to either of those abominable forces, but all has been occupied by Noise.

## Unit 7 (Chapter 27)

*Why* that creative act leaves room for their free will is the problem of problems, the secret behind the Enemy's nonsense about "Love." *How* it does so is no problem at all; for the enemy does not *foresee* the humans making their free contributions in a future, but *sees* them doing so in His unbounded Now. And obviously to watch a man doing something is not to make him do it.

## Unit 8 (Chapter 29)

Well, I am afraid it is no good trying to make him brave. Our research department has not yet discovered (though success is hourly expected) how to produce *any* virtue. This is a serious handicap. To be greatly and effectively wicked a man needs some virtue. What would Attila have been without his courage, or Shylock without self-denial as regards the flesh? But as we cannot supply these qualities ourselves we can only use them as supplied by the Enemy—and this means leaving Him a kind of foothold in those men whom, otherwise, we have made most securely our own.

## Unit 9 (*Screwtape Proposes a Toast*)

What I want to fix your attention on is the vast, overall movement towards the discrediting, and finally the elimination, of every kind of human excellence—moral, cultural, social, or intellectual. And is it not pretty to notice how *Democracy* (in the incantatory sense) is now doing for us the work that was once done by the most ancient Dictatorships, and by the same methods?

## ENRICHMENT ACTIVITIES

1. *The Screwtape Letters*, with its unique reversal of perspective, reveals many dangers and traps of evil and immorality that people face. However, this interesting perspective of Screwtape is limited, and thus provides an incomplete guide for living as a Christian. Based on the evil we are warned against in *The Screwtape Letters*, what is the good Lewis believes we should pursue? Feel free to draw from other writings of Lewis. Make an annotated list of the most important "goods." "Annotated" means that under the heading you would write some notes on what this means. For example:

   **Pleasure**

   *Screwtape chides Wormwood for allowing true pleasure to the patient b/c it reintroduces him to reality, helps him forget himself, and defends him against falseness and pride.*

   **Obedience**

   *Screwtape reminds Wormwood that a patient who is obedient even when he doesn't feel emotionally close to God (the Enemy) grows immeasurably in faith.*

2. *The Screwtape Letters* is dedicated to J.R.R. Tolkien, a close friend and another famous Inklings writer. Pick a lesson or theme from this book and illustrate its truth using a character of Tolkien's.

3. Write your own Screwtape letter! Write a Screwtape letter (from one demon to another) with the topic of how to deal with a patient. (See the appendix for sample Screwtape letters.) The patient shouldn't be people in general, but a particular individual—you perhaps, or someone you know. Develop your idea with the following in mind in terms of *content*:

   - The practical realities of living as this person in a specific place (sexuality, food, specific pain and pleasure, wasting time, churchgoing)
   - The psychological and spiritual issues that arise (repentance, humility, jokes, dim uneasiness, self-consciousness, unconsciousness, idolatry)
   - The philosophical or theological or political ideas/concepts that are grappled with by this person (love, historical Jesus, Marxism, democracy, eschatology, etc.)
   - Relationships that are useful in tempting the patient to sin (patient and his mother, patient and girlfriend, patient and superficial friends)

   Keep the following in mind for *formal* concerns:

   - Grammar and usage, punctuation, style
   - Tone of voice that your demon will use
   - Diction (word choice): remember, in *The Screwtape Letters*, the demons speak of the lowerarchy, Our Father Below, names of the demons, etc.
   - Figures of speech ("I have been in correspondence with Slumtrimpet who is in charge of your patient's young woman, and begin to see the chink in her armour" [129]; "It is as if a royal child whom his father has placed, for love's sake, in titular command of some great province, under the real rule of wise counsellors, should come to fancy he really owns the cities" [113]; "That it would peel off from his sensibility the kind of crust you have been forming on it, and make him feel that he was come home, recovering himself" [65])

- Plot and how it fits into the overall progress of this person's soul ("I note with great displeasure that the Enemy has, for the time being, put a forcible end to your direct attacks on the patient's chastity" [105])

4. Create an audio recording of one or more of the chapters from *The Screwtape Letters*. Experiment with tone and phrasing to emphasize the unique narrative perspective and to highlight important themes.

5. Throughout the *The Screwtape Letters*, sin is often cast as an exaggeration or minimization of God's intention. For example, when discussing God's gift of pleasure, Screwtape says, "All we can do is to encourage the humans to take the pleasures which our Enemy has produced, at times, or in ways, or in degrees, which He has forbidden" (44). Choose two to three other gifts from God, besides pleasure, and explain how they could become corrupted through exaggeration or minimization. In addition, explain in what manner these gifts should be enjoyed. Pick gifts relevant to your own life. Write this in annotated list form just as you did for question 1.

6. Go see *The Screwtape Letters* performed as a play.

7. Stage your own Screwtape Letters show after watching YouTube scenes of its Broadway production. Choose your favorite chapter and dramatize it your way. Once you've performed, explain your choices—which always involve critical decisions and judgment.

8. Read Franz Kafka's *The Metamorphosis* (available at gutenberg.org/files/5200/5200-h/5200-h.htm). How does its metaphor compare or contrast with the metaphor from *The Screwtape Letters* of the demon taking the shape of a centipede (letter 22)? Explain your conclusion.

# Great Ideas Theme-Gathering Essays

Now that you are nearing completion of this study, you will be asked to present Lewis's view on the great ideas in *The Screwtape Letters* in the form of an essay. We have provided a thesis for each great idea as well as questions that bring the themes of the course together. In the teacher's edition of the guide, we go on to give a sample of an argumentative essay for each theme. Your essay(s) should include textual support from different sections of the novel (quotes from Great Ideas Quotes pages you've completed), and you should also look for relevant excerpts from Lewis's context essays. In one to three pages, you should defend your thesis in an argumentative essay format (make an argument and support it with details and description as well as quotation and examples).

Our main goal here is to help you begin making connections and forming arguments about ideas that run throughout a book. You have sorted the pieces of the puzzle into piles of similar colors (by reading, marking the book, taking notes, answering questions, and having discussions); now you can put the puzzle together (the difference being a puzzle has one way to go together, but themes can be discussed and argued in endless ways). Please use our examples however they are useful to you. Choose a question that has particular significance in your own life—perhaps one that you have struggled with or has been particularly challenging in your own life or the life of your family. This will make your writing stronger and more purposeful.

## Tips for Writing a Great Essay

- Support your thesis with quotations from your Great Ideas Quotes pages.
- Support your thesis with the essays you read alongside this book.
- Develop your ideas with examples.
- Help us to see with description how your examples prove your argument.
- Explain your quotations and how they fit your argument.
- Consider what argument someone might make against yours and address those concerns as part of your defense.
- Conclude by restating your thesis with the depth of understanding you have established in the course of the writing.

## Theme Essay Question on *Real Pleasure*

Screwtape harshly scolds Wormwood for allowing the patient to read a book he simply enjoyed. He fears this real, positive pleasure because it is a touchstone (a standard by which to test) for reality.

### Question

How does real pleasure, such as reading a book you genuinely enjoy, bring you closer to God?

### Expanded Question

Explain how real pleasure works against Screwtape's goal of leading people away from God. Why does God want us to experience real pleasure?

### Thesis (feel free to choose your own)

**As God's invention, real pleasure serves God's purpose to replace lies with the truth of God's love for us as individuals and bring us into relationship with Him; pleasure brings us self-knowledge and humility, two conditions for coming into relationship with God.**

## Theme Essay Question on *Evil/Twisting the Good*

One recurring theme in Lewis's writing is the nature of evil. Lewis argues that evil cannot produce anything new, but just twist the existing good into a corrupted form. Often the pleasures of sin disguise the reality that sinful pleasure is a lesser substitute for pleasure as God intended it. Screwtape admits that real pleasure is God's invention, despite pleasure's role in temptation.

### Question

Real pleasure is God's invention, but pleasure can be twisted by the devil for other purposes. How does Screwtape use pleasure when tempting the patient?

### Expanded Question

How does Screwtape twist pleasure or offer a substitute, lesser pleasure to entrap the patient and others? If you have read it, consider comparing Screwtape's method of temptation with that of the White Witch from *The Lion, the Witch and the Wardrobe.*

### Thesis (feel free to choose your own)

**Satan succeeds in seducing our souls only when he can deceive us to accept a lesser substitute for what God has already graciously given. We see this motif in the relationship between Edmund and the White Witch in Narnia.**

## Theme Essay Question on *Relationships*

Screwtape and Wormwood pay close attention to the relationships in the patient's life. For example, when the patient develops friendships with rich, smart, and cynical people, Screwtape is delighted and encourages those friendships. In the relationship between the patient and his mother, Screwtape desires to produce conflict. Screwtape also hopes to isolate the patient from the community of the Church. Additionally, Screwtape and Wormwood discuss the patient's love interest and her family.

### Question

Describe two or three of the patient's relationships and how those relationships affect (or could have affected) the patient's faith.

### Expanded Question

Describe two or three of the patient's relationships and their effect on the patient. Why is Screwtape eager to promote some relationships over others? What potential do these relationships have to move the patient closer to God (the Enemy) or to hell (Our Father Below)?

### Thesis (feel free to choose your own)

**Screwtape understands the important role relationships play in the patient's life and works to undermine the patient's faith through relationships.**

## Theme Essay Question on *Time*

In "Time and Beyond Time," the essay on time that you read as a context essay, Lewis uses the metaphor of an author writing a book to help explain God's relationship to time. An author can write about a character for an hour, stop writing, and do something else. When he comes back, the author can continue writing as if no time passed for the character. The author remains outside the linear time line of the book. In *The Screwtape Letters*, Screwtape also describes God as having a special relationship to time that is different from the human relationship to it.

### Question

How does Lewis's metaphor of the author writing a book explain that God is not bound by our concept of linear time?

### Expanded Question

Screwtape notes that God does not foresee the future, but rather sees all action in "His unbounded Now" (150). How does Lewis's metaphor of the author writing a book help explain the "unbounded Now"? Compare the "unbounded Now" to our concepts of past, present, and future.

### Thesis (feel free to choose your own)

**Lewis illustrates his theory about God's perspective on time through the metaphor of a writer and his book.**

## Theme Essay Question on the *Gradual Road to Hell*

In his letters, Screwtape instructs Wormwood to appreciate the small sins: "Indeed the safest road to Hell is the gradual one—the gentle slope, soft underfoot, without sudden turnings, without milestones, without signposts" (61).

### Question

What does Screwtape mean by the "gradual, gentle slope," and why is the gradual decline into sin the safest road to hell?

### Expanded Question

What does Screwtape mean by the "gradual, gentle slope," and why is the gradual decline into sin the safest road to hell? What sins does Screwtape hope to include in the patient's gradual slope? What attitudes and actions does a gradual decline encourage or discourage?

### Thesis (feel free to choose your own)

**C.S. Lewis argues that the most common and most dangerous way for a person to wind up in hell is through small steps of disobedience, which we commit without any serious consideration of the consequences.**

## Theme Essay Question on *Emotion and Faith*

Screwtape begins the book warning Wormwood to avoid using reason to influence his patient. Instead, Screwtape often encourages attacks that capitalize on the patient's changing emotional state and feelings. One of the greatest blows to Screwtape's agenda occurs when a Christian who does not feel like obeying God chooses to obey nevertheless.

### Question

How does Screwtape use the patient's emotions to try to attack his faith?

### Expanded Question

How does emotion influence the development of faith, and how does Screwtape attempt to attack the patient's faith through emotion? Does this invalidate our emotions in relationship to our faith? You may want to consider the patient's attempts at prayer and his response to the war.

Please use both *The Screwtape Letters* and the essay "Faith" from *Mere Christianity* in your response.

### Thesis (feel free to choose your own)

**Lewis argues that the changing nature and power of emotions can become a stumbling block for Christians, or can teach us to persevere through the peaks and troughs of our feelings.**

## Theme Essay Question on the *Individual Soul*

Lewis set *The Screwtape Letters* during World War II. This war consumed the European continent and affected all aspects of life there. World War II was the deadliest military conflict in history with over 60 million people killed. As a young British man, the patient would have been shaped by World War II as he faced issues of the draft, rationing, and repeated bombings over Britain. As you know, the patient loses his very life because of this war.

### Question

Screwtape often scolds Wormwood for his delighted obsession with the war. Screwtape continually redirects Wormwood's focus to the state of the patient's soul. Why does Screwtape value the fate of an individual's soul over the fate of nations or countries?

### Expanded Question

Although the World War II remains one of the most significant, century-defining events of history, Screwtape often scolds Wormwood for his delighted obsession with the war. Screwtape continually redirects Wormwood's focus to the state of the patient's soul. If Screwtape discusses the war (such as the debate between pacifism and patriotism), it is only because the issues affect the patient's moral choices. Why does Screwtape value the fate of an individual's soul over the fate of nations or countries? Contrast Screwtape's goal for individuals with God's desire for the individual person. Why is God concerned with people *as individuals*? What is God's ultimate goal for humanity, according to the emphasis of *The Screwtape Letters*?

### Thesis (feel free to choose your own)

**In *The Screwtape Letters*, Lewis presents God as chiefly concerned with individual people, over and against nations, and committed to individuals becoming the fullest version of themselves.**

# Appendix: Sample Screwtape Letters

In the Enrichment Activities we recommend writing your own Screwtape letter particular to your circumstances. In fact, this would be a fine substitute for the theme-gathering essay. The following "Screwtape letters" were written at the college level. The students generously gave permission for them to be included here.

*My dearest Slumdredge,*

I am glad that you brought to my attention your situation. Of course I have been keeping tabs on you, but I write to you now to highlight the gravity of the situation in which you find yourself. Your subject, as he has chosen to remain a student at a Christian college, inherits certain defenses. However, do not be disheartened, for anything can be manipulated to work for Our Father Below. Once, when I worked at a lowly post similar to yours (although not *as* low), I encountered a subject very similar to the boy you are dealing with now. His biggest weakness proved to be his confusion, and that is what I suggest you prod at now. For you see, confusion leads to doubt, and doubt can seep into even the most secure areas. If correctly handled, his foundations will shake. You will be as water in concrete when the frost comes. Slowly you will burrow until he is cracked and yet sees himself as whole.

Ah, but let me cut to the chase, for time spent dawdling could lose us the soul. An important thing to remember is not to become overwhelmed with points of attack. Start at one place and establish yourself. An easy example is his confidence. It is bolstered by petty achievements and small successes. The Enemy loves this type of general confidence because it does not consume the subject but gives strength previously unnoticed. Strength such as this must be taken away. These little victories need to grow. They need to define him. However, be warned. This process needs subtle execution. For if he sees the building of an unhealthy confidence from small feats he will laugh at himself. He will say, "What have I done really?" and progress will be lost.

Another powerful tool of yours is separation of thought. No matter how good an idea, if isolated it does very little good to its procreator. You must not let him bring together inspiration from the Enemy with its application to his life. His mind must be muddled and dark or filled with static that mixes signals and ideas. The hope is that he will not be able to recognize this interference, but at the very least we want his mind to stall so that he becomes disheartened at his inability to think. If the latter is the case, it has been common for us to use people of his ability for great deeds in our favor. (My director once worked with Heinrich Himmler.) The static becomes so profound that erratic conclusions are formed and the tools that were given to him by the Enemy become assets for Our Father of the Deep.

I saw in your last letter that the subject is not as consumed with lust as we would like. It seems obvious that you haven't been doing your job, especially during this era of flesh and infidelity. We have worked hard to push societal norms towards promiscuity and even harder to ensure that the idea of morality loses objectivity. Once a human decides that its only boundaries are those that it wants, the game is up. For what do humans know of light and dark? They are like infant rodents whose eyes are not yet open. As they stumble towards subjective morality, they inch closer to their consumption. To say the least, then, you must instill in your subject the idea of "What is right for me may not be the same as what is right for him," or "The church is outdated. Besides, it gives guidelines more than anything." At that moment our grip will strengthen twofold. A man who has no boundaries has already allowed himself to be coaxed into almost anything.

I warn you again that this must be a gradual process. The idea is to start with lust for his neighbor (if only briefly) and eventually, without him knowing it, begin to see nothing else. Take note, my pupil, for it is hard to understand these humans; we only have one hunger, but they have many. We have the means to overdevelop one hunger so that eventually it dictates the others. Lust becomes the filter through which all else flows. It becomes not only a desire but also a mind-set, and then the reins become shorter. You have the ability to prod at one desire and cause a ripple of sin throughout his being. When that happens your patient shall truly be in hand.

On a bit of a different note I would like to discuss purpose. As I mentioned, the confusion of your subject holds great importance in winning his soul. Confusion about smaller items, much of the time, leads to a confusion of purpose. This can be a slippery slope for humans. I would suggest separating him from what he knows and pushing him to change unnecessarily. Help him to ignore the gifts the Enemy has given to him and instead seek the gifts of others. Through this he will not only fail (or at least struggle) but also become focused on something other than the aim we need to avoid (the Enemy). Let him get caught up in the need for temporal success and forget that eternity exists. Humans are susceptible to living for the moment (which regrettably can benefit them if they rely on the Enemy), so if you give him things to do constantly he will become bogged down. Time to think or reflect does not benefit our cause, so I encourage you to avoid it at all costs. Items like money, friendship, family, and even love can blind him from what we know. You might say, "Those things do not harm humans," but what you must understand is that these items begin to act as blinders. They work for the Enemy if in their proper place and through this they are powerful tools at our disposal. For if they are confused, how will they recognize proper love from tainted love? Blur definitions of commonly good items and a new sword you wield.

Most importantly, I suggest that you stay tireless in your work. My career exemplifies this perfectly. I rose through the ranks consistently and quickly because my voraciousness exceeded others'. Now I work constantly filing important complaint notices. Apparently humans do not favor being consumed. Ah, but I digress again, so let me state my point clearly. The Enemy never rests. He never ceases. He never waivers. Be as waves upon His cliffs, powerful and fierce, or subtle and unrelenting, as a stream that forms a canyon. Either way, vigilance is necessary at all times, and I remind you that you will pay the price for negligence. We are hungry in the depths and our sustenance must come from somewhere, whether it is you or your patient.

*Sincerely,*

Thumbletwarn

Head of the Office of Complaints and Inquires Below (HOCIB)

*P.S. Research & Development almost had a breakthrough today corrupting prayer. No success.*

*My dear brother Scumteeth,*

Congratulations on the overwhelming success of your last patient—there were a few tense moments where I didn't think you could pull him through, but you shocked us all here in Eternal Affairs. Who could have anticipated that your very first assignment would be so fruitful? I mean, not only did you manage to drive your man into a beautiful, filthy addiction, but just think of all the carnage you wreaked on his sniveling little family. Beetgrin owes you a share of his next commission for the psychological number your man did on those little spawn he calls his children. But I shouldn't have been surprised; after all, greatness seems to run in our family.

But don't get too cocky just yet, rookie. Do you think I got where I am today by celebrating one victory (and if I may modestly remind you, I contributed invaluable coaching to that one) while my next assignment skipped blissfully into the Enemy's eager, sweaty hands? No. Stay focused.

I ran the name of your next assignment in our newly updated database (ah, Updates. What a genius concoction from Our Father Below, a new name for that perpetual hunger of Innovation), and while I normally advise against preemptive celebration, you must be rejoicing in your subject's situation: a college student. Do you know how much sweet, keening Noise she walks in day after day? She wades through body images, trash e-mails, advertisements (those desperate whores in the clutches of our brilliant Trend Specialists), and mindless bureaucratic errands just to get from her desk to her front door.

There's a tactic we've been working on for ages, and while it wanes in the strangely united aftermath of events foolish humans call Tragedies (don't they know that Death scoops them out of our reach?), it's been largely successful since the beginning. These herdish creatures are pack animals, and from the minute of their sticky, mewling birth they seek connections with one another, bafflingly. And while we are often able to manipulate this insipid urge to unite in thought, it is even more profitable to split them up. In that lumpy island where you're stationed (they call it the United States), we've seen skyrocketing success in this area. Our operatives work along the lines of the strategy employed by hyenas (noble creatures)—identify the limp-legged and aged, and once separated from the rest of the waddling mass, pinch and snap at the ankles of the straggler till she falls.

We get away with this so easily by the manipulation of what those "United" States are obsessed with: freedom. What a triumph for us, to twist that disgusting idea of the Enemy's that man might think for himself. With the cry of Independence, we've convinced them to isolate, to individualize. Headphones, BlackBerrys, closed doors, cubicles, the idea of "personal space": these are the fruits of our tireless noble labors. And every self-seeking act is predicated in the name of their lofty capitalism. I'm getting intoxicated; let's get back to business here.

Once you have extracted her from the pack, you will find it's much easier to loose bolts in her brain. You see what you've got to work with—convince your patient that on that whimpering, wind-blown hill in the middle of nowhere, she is a sophisticate far above what you can get her to call the "typical student." Never mind the Enemy's dull insistence that every human is varicolored and just bursting with personality; get her to see that every one of these sappy mudsuckers is the same, unfashionable lazy slob with hollow opinions and a boring taste in music.

Ah, that brings me to one of my favorites. Twisting Taste, that facet of Pleasure into something tangible and effective—if we put them in competition even in their Pleasures (and I don't mean that worthless competition of "sport," but the real stuff, the thrill of blood beneath fingernails, the sweet smell of pretentious judgment), an even wider wedge can be driven between each of them. Your gal is a sucker for Taste. It seems great to them at first ("What's wrong with befriending people with common interests?"), but if you play it right, it can quickly descend our way into exclusion of those who don't share those little Pleasures. She'll become so ready to dislike anything she's not familiar with, and her previous tempter has so blurred the line between the person and his interests, that for her there is no distinguishing. This blurry line is vital to our schemes, and a perfect illustration of how our idea of Categories has stuck, quivering potently like a dart in a board.

Now, you know that the Enemy is the master of Order, that dull routine humdrum of everything having a place and a role, and that our gracious Father has bestowed the gift of Chaos, our special freedom. Our Categories are the facsimile to Order, a cruel trick to get humans to excuse Judgmentalism by way of "making sense of things." It's another way to dissipate the pack, really—they're ready enough to form groups of like-minded breeds; it's only one step between including new members and excluding the undesirables. To the glee of the folks in Eternal Affairs, Stereotype caught like a match to newspaper, and is just as effective at breaking down communication. With Categories, each man makes up his mind about another person and contrives a face for the person he will meet. With those masks assigned to one another, people meet each other on all falsity and assumption, and Our Father Below sighs contentedly, assured that no rebellion of united beings is at risk.

So you have a lot to work with. Still, it surprises me that the Lower Downs would assign you this post; as if you knew the female human brain, as if you could wriggle into its crannies and scoop out gleaming insecurities from the depths. Don't you worry about this. I will be giving you precise instructions for such treasures as body image, gossip, and vanity. I also remember from my correspondence with her former attendant that she could be a handful whenever she summoned the energy to be one. I don't know if they told you what happened to Mudmilk that brought an end to their professional relationship, but after an incident involving the choice of college for the little brat, an incident during which Mudmilk had been sleeping off a month-long hangover and missed her chance to discourage a Christian college (on the basis of "all the Hypocrisy" she'd undoubtedly discover there), Mudmilk was "reassigned" to a new sector in the Eternal Affairs. I hear M.M. filled the long-vacant position of sweeping up the bones from our Father's feast-table. At least she managed to make the girl's first semester delightfully hellish, packed with fear, doubt, and nightmares. I am surrounded by incompetent idiots who are only interested in moving down the ladder.

A shame about her boyfriend. He goes against everything you're aiming for, dear brother. He has this nasty way of distracting her focus, so carefully pinpointed, away from herself. And worse, directs it off himself too—if only you were that lucky. The best way to twist anything the Enemy's built is to Magnify it, for as your distant relation Undersecretary Screwtape (TE, BS, etc.) used to say, "All extremes, except extreme devotion to the Enemy, are to be encouraged." If you can make this incessant grounding presence in her life something of an idol, you will have made me proud to be your sister. For the best types of sins are the misguided virtues. The best part is that our golden calf will feel the immense pressure of her divine expectations, and the deep-reaching disappointment for both when he naturally fails to meet them will serve delightfully to drive them apart. This sort of slope is gradual, so for the time being, encourage in every way you can their disgusting act of breeding. Cultivate in her a sour mixture of overwhelming want and guilty shame about the whole act so that even when it's finally granted (whether in the flimsy, useless construct of Marriage or not), the whole idea will be so muddled that she'll say sophisticatedly over coffee, "It's really quite overrated. I'd much rather read a good book."

So don't fret too much about the boyfriend as a threat; if you cooperate with his demon, the two of you can erode their stronghold. Just remember that humans are always stronger as a crowded, stinking pack, so do all you can to wither them apart from each other. I would say that Relationships are the greatest threat to our design, and their greatest tool against our sweet, tremendous pall. Luckily, for the most part the creatures are unaware of the power they collect in every household, and turn biting against each other.

My last word (I'm on my way to a summit on Innovative Nightmares): for your girl, keep her moving. When she's at rest, all this pesky Imagination spills out onto various sheets of paper, and the satisfied smirk of the Enemy at this insipid pursuit is vomit-inducing. (Remember the difference between Reverie and Imagination—Reverie is our special brand of Time Wasting in which not even the body moves as the brain sags like a rotting tree in August, while Imagination has the obscene reek of insects imitating their Creator.) The best way to consume her attention is with an overlapping, intricate to-do list. She will attempt to keep afloat with well-intentioned time management, but be ruthless. Give her meaningless errand after meaningless errand to chase after, convince her that she's "got to" get it all done, that she can take a walk tomorrow, that she can read for fun on the weekend. "Work now, play later" is so effective if you can make the work never-ending.

Be on your pointed toes at all times. All humans are tricky, and I have a suspicion they might be receiving Outside Help, the little cheaters.

*Your beloved sister,*

Skinflint

[First Citizen of the Deep Dark Lord, Director of the Torture Board, Chairwoman of Education]

*My dear Sneersnout,*

You whining, insolent gnat! How dare you question the lowerarchy's decision? I am grieved to hear that one of *my* underlings has been grumbling to other putrid recent Tempter University graduates about his, and I quote, "wholly unsalvageable and demeaning assignment." Did you honestly believe Our Father's Below's personal Morale Agency vigilantes would not hear your pathetic attempts to garner sympathy? Your womanish laments nauseate me. Fortunately for you, I will forgo pressing charges with the Correctional Courts and spare you twenty-three centuries of torture and incarceration. Beware, however: memory of such unprofessional behavior does not easily fade and I lovingly caution you to avoid following in the footsteps of your predecessor, Ergbed, whose idiocy did not lessen the sweet nectar of his will.

Read carefully your patient's folder. Beginner mishaps and lack of information are inadequate excuses for botched cases. I fear your first report has revealed a severe lack of patient knowledge. However, I shall continue writing under the assumption you have now burned the information onto your brain with the gleeful impulsion of Vermbite when he brands his newest crop of so-called Pharisees.

Yes, my naive graduate, "Pharisees" still exist in the Enemy's camp today. This is what endows hope to your assignment. Never write off a lifelong Christian. Those furthest in the Enemy's camp taste the sweetest when converted. Your patient, regrettably an Enemy agent since childhood, can become our trophy Pharisee or better yet, Blasphemer. Hope remains for your patient.

You boisterously bemoan the academic nature of your student and her satisfactory transition to college life, wishing like other demons to drown your patient with hatred of school, corrupt her disposition, and ruin her college experience, which all would hopefully result in the patient gloriously cursing the Enemy. Yet you barely mentioned that your patient is actually surprised by the amount of reading and writing her classes demand! What did Dubdud teach you idiots in the University? Tempting 101: Encourage and exploit misconceptions. Seize the opportunity afforded by this surprise.

By all outward appearances, your patient is adjusting splendidly to the college workload, but her internal confidence waivers. Praise to Our Father Below that her elder sister's mantra was "College was easier for me, work-wise, than high school." Thankfully, your patient stupidly believed this individual experience would apply to her. Perhaps the only success of your predecessor was convincing the patient that her eleven AP classes meant she'd breeze through college. Exploit this misconception and constantly remind her how hard and time-consuming her classes are. Stir in her a sense of inferiority. Although the patient considered herself the smartest of her three siblings (a useful, and mouthwatering morsel of pride), let the mountains of work convince her she is academically inept.

Root your attack strategy in feelings, for the logic is absurd. (Seventeen credits, including three writing-intensive classes, would translate to many hours of studying no matter how bright the student.) Keep her preoccupied with the feeling of disappointment and she won't realize the truth. Oh, and don't forget to throw in the thought that "the College (its abominable name would make me puke if mentioned) was supposed to be the easier school." Mock your patient. Tell her she struggles at the "dumb-downed" college. Of course, that this despicable institution is a slacker college is a lie, a silly connotation developed over years of siblings lauding the academic nature of their Other College and fostered by her sickening admiration for family. Let us use her own silly notion and develop a deep disappointment and disgust with herself.

However, rein in your diabolical enthusiasm and refrain from introducing such zany ideas like depression or self-destructive behavior. Your patient knows those landmarks well enough and will quickly become aware of your influence and our whole attack shall crumble. Moreover, also avoid cataclysmic spirit-crushing. Don't make her desperate enough to run to God, an annoying past tendency of your patient. Plague her with self-doubt, but kindle her pride. Never let her admit her struggles to others. Entwine her with vines of false notions. Let her believe any academic failure from a Christian scholar would dishonor God, and convince her that a truly intelligent Christian student handles academic hurdles with silent grace. You will simultaneously tear away her sense of her intrinsic value while cementing the false pride the Enemy tries in vain to abolish.

Speaking of confidence bulldozers, why did you not inform me earlier of the roommate's beauty? Did you believe only attractive members of the opposite sex can fuel temptations? You forget how comparison-driven these rotten humans are. Every time your patient looks at the roommate, point out how pretty the roommate is. Draw attention to the "better aspects" that the patient wishes she could posses, like her better smile, her better shaped legs, even her better height. Page 745 in the patient's file should detail how well we exploited this physical attribute in childhood. Sometimes old "healed" hurts profit us more splendidly when reopened. Your incompetent twit of a predecessor, Ergbed, would tearfully screech that the patient could successfully repel this attack by quoting from the poisonous-fumed psalm, "I praise you because I am fearfully and wonderfully made." You, however, must not be so weak. Many of my students have overcome worse. Pulpsoot once drove a mediating monk to murder with a continuous hailstorm of hate-filled thoughts, and your patient isn't nearly as biblically knowledgeable. Fail not to see the gaping whole in this scriptural armor. Nail her on one physical aspect not intended by God—her weight. How fortunate that she, like most of our American cases, flops around with rolls of excess fat.

Compassionately, I warn you to approach this issue with trepidation and a suitable dose of fear. Here, we have experienced our greatest victories for the Lowly Kingdom in her life, but also our most ignoble defeats. It was for Ergbed's colossal failure in this regard that he was finally relieved of duty and devoured. Ergbed egged her gluttony on, too much, too fast, and the shock was enough to wake the patient up from the slumber we so patiently lulled her in. The patient realized her hypocrisy in citing "the body is the temple of the Holy Spirit" when rebuffing sexual or alcoholic sins, yet stuffing her face with no regard to the effect on her body. Oh, those glorious months when she did not control what she ate, but through food we controlled her. Her eating habits were our leash and harness for her spiritual life. We steered her further and further from the Enemy's path. But alas! She has committed that horrible act, so distastefully described as "repentance."

Before you, snippety shrimp, scamper stupidly off to the Demonology prosecutors, I mention this unfortunate event, not to recollect the Enemy's victory, but to full-heartedly convince you that body comparing is the issue to push here. The patient is now acutely sensitive to how her body outwardly appears. As she wrestles with her physical identity "in the Enemy," shrink-wrap her soul with a judgmental and critical attitude. Impale her mind with this false theological javelin: outward appearances correlate with a person's relationship strength with the Enemy. Twist the Enemy's propagandist metaphor of a "new creation" and help her elevate physical regeneration over the spiritual. Prod her to scoff and sigh as she sees behemoth-bodied students smother their lunch trays with grease-oozing food. Spoil her soul with a superiority complex, but consume her corporal form with unsatisfiable longing for that same lard-laden food.

Encourage her to compare her eating successes and failures to her compatriots. Plant the seeds of jealously and cultivate the tree of envy until it overshadows every single interaction, especially as it concerns the pretty roommate. Our long-term goal in this roommate relationship is for jealousy to lead to hatred and hatred to cruelty. Yet increase your patient's struggle to eat healthfully. Her diet is in vain because she is unable to control how the fatty fools at the college cafeteria prepare food. Perhaps it will prove beneficial for you to be in contact with Mudglub, the roommate's tempter. He is skilled weaver of subtle destructive actions. Your attack's effectiveness will increase tenfold if the roommate decides to eat ice cream at every meal. This small deviation, something the roommate would never consider a sin, might have major beneficial repercussions for your patient.

In addition to physical jealously, a pretty roommate provides us the opportunity to pursue boyfriend issues. When you write Mudglub, encourage him to foster any romantic relationships for the pretty girl. The speedier the better. Not only will speed provide ample opportunities for Mudglub to tempt the roommate, but it will also force your patient to confront the issue of intimate relationships. After you contact Mudglub, send me a report on the roommate's relationship status and the romantic situations of all girls on their hall, and I shall advise you with more precise information.

*Your magnanimous mentor,*

Chokewhip

# Notes

Notes

# Notes

Classical Subjects…

# the art of POETRY

…Creatively Taught

*"There has never been a civilization without poetry…*

…Poetry acknowledges something deep within our nature—an urge to name, say, sing, grieve, praise, out of our solitariness, to another person. It makes words into a material thing, hard and solid as a table, dense with significance."

—from the Introduction

by Christine Perrin
Director of Writing,
Messiah College

*The Art of Poetry* teaches the practice of reading a poem slowly and carefully, introducing students to the elements of poetry and the many forms that a poem can take, from sonnet to open verse. In the belief that practice is the best way to learn, this excellent curriculum for upper-middle school and high school students is rich with explications, exercises, and activities.

**Full Program Includes:**

- *The Art of Poetry Student Edition*
- *The Art of Poetry Teacher's Edition*
- *The Art of Poetry Streaming Video* (or DVD Set)

Pairs perfectly with *Bright Mirror*, a book of 53 poems by Christine Perrin!

Free samples at
www.ClassicalAcademicPress.com

# WALKING TO WISDOM

LITERATURE GUIDE SERIES

*Stories* give us an experience of certain knowledge, which is why how we feel about the book is part of what the book is teaching us. We have kept this in mind while making the Walking to Wisdom Literature Guides, to be used in conjunction with the works of C.S. Lewis, J.R.R. Tolkien, and Dorothy Sayers. Each literature guide both stands on its own and interacts with the others, with sidebar comments and thematic continuity. These books will change students' lives and, in the meantime, teach them how to read with delight, depth, and skill.

**Our literature guides thoughtfully instill students with the following habits:**

- taking notes in their books
- answering reading questions and creating their own questions
- keeping notes book-wide on themes and motifs
- answering discussion questions about thematic material
- memorizing important quotations
- preparing, while reading, to write
- participating in creative enrichment activities related to the books

"I believe that a large part of the value of reading great books is wrestling with the ideas and stories, and this series seems to be one of the best I've ever seen for accomplishing this." —Cathy Duffy

www.ClassicalAcademicPress.com